Clicks and Clangs
(Prosody)

Uzoma Nduka (Ph.D.).

First Edition

Copyright ©2022 Dr Uzo Nduka
All rights reserved.

Published by The Lighthouse books, Agape Inc.

All rights reserved. No part of this publication may be used or reproduced in any manner whatsoever without the written permission except in the case of brief quotations embedded in critical articles and reviews. Requests for permission should be addressed to the Lighthouse Books editor at editor@thelighthousebooks.com

For more information regarding permission, write to:
The Lighthouse Books, 13721 E. Rice Pl, Aurora,
CO 80015.

Cover Image inspired by Ekele Nwabuisi and designed by Nonso Ugwuoke.

ISBN: 978-1-950320-37-0 [Paperback]
ISBN: 978-1-950320-38-7 [Digital]

Visit us at:
www.thelighthousebooks.com
Printed in the USA

Contents

i hear clicks and clangs 1
let me tell you 1
then when... 3
subdued? 5
st. paul's message..8
epistle. mine? 10
i spoke 11
unfaithfulness..12
double edged sword 13
i was like you 14
the end 16
amen..17
you all *effed*..18
we make the dead roll 19
we all need a good editor 20
don't call me black...21
wake up, my giant, wake up..22
that's the name you choose 23
i didn't leave you, you left me...24
2020...26
until we all die 27
oppressors narcissism 28
beast..29

beavers are better	30
letter to Covid	31
let's pray?	33
what do you see?	37
woe!	38
as it was in the beginning	40
blurry countess in the canyon	41
all are Bolingbrook	42
sifter (1)	44
sifter (11)	46
sifter (iii)	48
i don't know how to ride a bike	49
all these years	50
as you go into	52
wounded duck	53
i see many universe	56
in the spirit, the spirit	57
half staff (1)	58
half staff (2)	59
to you all	61
no amen	64
then when	65

i hear clicks and clangs

i hear clicks and clangs
as the mechanic fiddles with his pliers and breaker bars
i hear bursts and bangs
as the Uberman drives down towns in screeching tires and screaming times
i hear pangs and clinging fangs as moms in rural Arkansas delivers to an unknown future
i hear the onomatopoeia from clicking *Ogene* sound and the talking drums of Ezeoke
i hear grill and broil as men barbecue their time away in frills and thrills
i hear tingling and tickling but not from otitis media but a clear head
i hear clamps and damps from the hallowed house of the people
i hear these and that not as a deranged but with a discerning mind
i hear these and that not as arising from a nightmarish meeting but as alert as a cat
i hear booms and dooms from the corners of inner cities and crevices of mid-towns
i hear sounds like a fiery wind in my ears
i hear them erupt from within like a psychotic
but assured that these rambunctious waters will settle for she has solid pores and unswerving walls.

let me tell you

let me tell you
this thing y'all call
squirrel, is called *uze* in my village.
we use it as
meat not a pet
it fills the stomach
and satisfies the soul.
it is a waste
in this your land
like Emmanuel *Obiakpolam* who
was the hunter described
in Chinua Achebe's Things
Fall Apart, he
never aimed to shoot
he just shoots and
they all come crashing
just like you do
now. you bring down
whoever you want to
you kill the effervescence
of the wretched world
you show them carrots
but stops the Pavlov's
cycle as soon as

they eject their artistry
and you pin them
down with your trademark
dog whistles and sorts
for this story has
always been your history.

then when...

this is when i
hate this thing-life.
when I see the
moon dropping on my
head and brats circle
around a bald man
who sits on a
wooden rocking chair telling
tales made by him.

this is what I hate:
that we have all
abandoned our yam porridge
and chased after marmalade
made with unfamiliar taste
jammed into our tastebuds
unlike the days of
old when we soaked
tubers into spicy red
oil and nodded our
sweating heads in approval.

this is why I hate
all these things-life

for we cannot change
the clock hands to
start when we want
and stop when we
are not moving forward
for we have to
move along with the
tick tock of life
or die when its
battery has all died.

subdued?

you think the
world is fair
and is just
take a trip
to Park Ave
when you return
tell the world
what you saw.

you think if
you work hard
and do all
things so right
that you will
get by easily
welcome to my
sweet lonely world
where you will
know what life
is truly like
even when you
have work so
so so hard
and done all

things so right

myths of this
nasty brutish world
lies told over
and over and
over and they
became part of
our changing lives
deceit of the
elites on those
on the fringes
of this world

do things right
work so hard
you'll get by
not so quickly
not so fast
not just real
for the forces
will toss your
brittle tails around
spank you on
all falling sides
till you break
into tiny little
pieces and they

still make mince
meat of you.

st. paul's message

(dedicated to Bishop Isreal Ade Ajala)
fellow elites,
trust me in this.
listen to this lone voice.
all these lazy ones want.
all these tomorrow's future want.
is the best.
the best for this motherland:
liberation! nothing less.
they want it with all in them.
they wound their knees in daily supplication for this.
they know we are energetically enthusiastic about god.
our own gods.
but, they also know that we have been doing everything exactly backwards.
they know that we have set up shops right across the streets.
they know that we have registered this land with foreign treasuries.
they know that we have stored away the finest fruits of tomorrow in personal warehouses.
and, we, unashamedly noisily hawk our stupidity in overt glare.
after all these years of refusing to refurbish our sensibilities.
after all these years of recalcitrantly recoiling our sacred nation.
after all these years of shoplifting our own dear sweat and blood.
we have all failed to hoist our head high.

we have all failed to smile and scream for our nativeland.
we have all failed and have nothing to show for our diverse tongues and tribes.
and the unity in diversity has turned its tongue against us.
now, our teeth are set on edge.
and we are scampering for safe haven.
listen to me my fellow bourgeois.
all these street urchins want is the best for the country they hail.

epistle. mine?

i have done what i ought to do.
i have met all the standards set.
i have checked all the right boxes.
i have met all the goals.
but, in all these, i have not succeeded.
i went to the right schools.
i read the right courses.
i scored A's in every subject.
i checked all the right boxes.
yet, the odds have not been on my side.

i spoke

i spoke when they called me black
because I am not black
i spoke when they called me un-evolved
because I am not un-evolved
i spoke when they mocked my accent
because they too have accent
i spoke when they called me shithole
because they too are shithole
and I will keep speaking
until this game is over

unfaithfulness

i was kidnapped by her rhetoric
i was hoodwinked by her heresy
i was deceived with her smooth talk
i was beguiled by her mistruths
i couldn't do much
because i didn't know much
i primitively thought she was honest
i timidly felt she had my back
it's now i know
she came from my back
and stabbed me through the back
and tore my being into tribes and tongues
i truly thought
she was on my side
but she tore through me without mercy

double edged sword

you heard him say he is a Graber
you shut your ears
because he protects the Evangelicals
you saw him siphon so much money
you closed your eyes
because you did not elect a Pope
you saw him sign that children be caged
you became blind
because you were not once an Immigrant
you heard him say he will not leave peacefully
you became deaf
because you so not enjoy democracy
you saw his tugs try to run a bus off the road
and you turned away your eyes
because you are a tug too
you heard him mock medical doctors and a man with congenital condition
and you kept quiet
because you have a jaundiced mind and deranged brain
you fell in line and fell in love
because you sold your soul to an already sold soul
we have seen were your loyalty lies: not in your country
but in you.

i was like you

so stupid
and naive
not knowing
what goes on
in the intestines
of other climes.

i was just like you
following the crowd
and chanting songs
i never knew
their meanings and
their origins.

i was like you
uninformed about
unincorporated landmarks
that exists
in the wombs
we cheer and roose.

i was just like you
so stupid
so naive

chanting songs
i never knew
their origins.

the end

we are not afraid of standing in the wind with our nakedness
we are not scared of frying this cake with the red rum running in and out of our veins
we are not afraid of dining with the vipers, the black mambas, the boomslangs with our chopped fingers
for we have nothing else to loose but to loose what we have already lost
we have broken our backs carrying your sins and your tattered totes
we have burned our woods with veiled lantern and inactive oil
we have... we have...
we have dwelt and wept and left
we have sulked and sobbed and squalled
we have... we have... we have
we have worn the crown of thorns
but raised our heads from your tomb
and ready to face the blue sky and rain judgements on you.

amen

we are not afraid of standing in the wind with our nakedness
we are not scared of frying this cake with the red rum running in and out of our veins
we are not afraid of dining with the vipers, the black mambas, the boomslangs with our chopped fingers
for we have nothing else to lose but to lose what we have already lost
we have broken our backs carrying your sins and your tattered totes
we have burned our woods with veiled lantern and inactive oil
we have... we have...
we have dwelt and wept and left
we have sulked and sobbed and squalled
we have... we have... we have
we have worn the crown of thorns
but raised our heads from your tomb
and ready to face the blue sky and rain judgements on you.

you all *effed*

why did you have to wear white
when you had raffia that's close to nature?
why did you have to speak with the nose
when you had the best flute in your guttural?
why did you have to exchange your own for shekels
when you should have used your own to make more barter?
why did you throw away your signposts of truth
when they came to you with unholy word of their mouth?
tell us why.

we make the dead roll

in our words
in our deeds

the seeds we sow
and debts we owe

in our hearts
and our acts

all we do
is kill the

soul of our
own hands.

we all need a good editor

like verse
and ryhmes
in ink
and pen

crossed at
times and
lighted high
we

sometimes need
an editor
to dot our
eyes and cross

our teeths
so we can see
what's good what's bad
and spew those things

not good as cods
we sometimes
need a
good deskman.

don't call me black

don't call me black
i'm not in anyway dusk
look at this charcoal
then, take a look at me
do we look like clones?
don't we look apart?
and this kettle too
do we share same surname?
stop throwing names around
and running with one that sticks
stop conjuring spirits
with your dog whistles
see my brother Jesus
whom you painted white
we came from same manger
the cradle for glorious people
you've called this lie for too long
and taken us for so much rides
the back is gently opening
with strong wind from the east
where the wisemen came from
don't call me black
for i'm not like dusk.

wake up, my giant, wake up

wake up, my giant, wake up
see the glory around you
see the gold that surround you
arise above the noises
arise beyond your nose
sprout like hibiscus
shine like the stars
rise like a flour
blow like a flute
stretch out like a fire
jerk and tweak and tug
push in like a fire
force through like a horse
tear down all the wedges
race through all the valleys
throttle down the alleys
for the time is ripe and now

that's the name you choose

you call yourself white
saying you are snow
where i can come and ski
so you are the avalanche
that eats its naive visitors
and drown their soaring visions
in swamps of hungry lions
you call yourself white
saying you are sepulcher
sycophant of the holy trinity
and Judas among apostles
that's the name you choose
that's what it all says.

i didn't leave you, you left me

you turned the house upside down
and set it all on fire
you pulled the wools over my eyes
and set my teeth on edge
you gave me scorpion and not fish
you left me dangling from the skies
you strained my legs with jiggers
and stuffed my throat with so much bile
during the great battle-
the Battle of our Soul-
you sold me to non-neighbors-
those who spoke differently-
you sent your shells and artilleries
to blow up my rugged skin
you stoked the kids against we two
and told them too that i've been wayward
you also said i'm a nuisance
in the glare of the sun
you shred me down
not one leaf
was left to shed
till today you still shun me
even when i've sang your praise
up till today you shut your ears

but shot my heart with your armor
you laid your boulders on my neck
and used your shoulders to shove it down
i had no choice
but to tie the nuptials
with the one who once raped me.

2020

man and money, dropping like autumn leaves
with wintry water dripping down cheeks and chokes
hoping you end with singing
certain you will end with sorrows
unknown to us, unknown to them
unknown to all that stepped into you
like whitened wintry stems, most will breath in
cast crispy air that comes with new moon.

until we all die

until we all die
oh! lord. not God.
your creation has sinned against you
they have also sinned against your spirit
the first Adam has mortally mauled humanity
each day, ears tingle
news jingle tears apart heart
lo, brother rise against brother
brown bounces billet on black
people pillage streets unleashing displaced dispraise
they tread on serpents and scorpions
but remain bitten by those they obey
oh! lord. not God.
your footstool has failed
your handiwork has desecrated your handsome works
we worth any of your glory?

oppressors narcissism

the waves were as huge as the mountains
screaming across seas and seasons
the shout was as loud as the thunder
warning signs of doomsday
written in plain sight
explained with naked mind
the braille told the untold story
hanging in bright blue skies for all to see.

not here, not there

sometimes i feel you built me up
sometimes i feel you crushed my feet
sometimes i feel you don't have ears
sometimes i feel your eyes have been drowned
sometimes i feel you aren't my lineage
sometimes i feel you had me for sales
sometimes i see my feelings distraught
sometimes i see my distraught destroyed
but most times i know not in my world
but most times i know more mouths will also see.

beast

i came to you,
not so willingly.
but forced down from
the shaking center.

in my naive mind,
i felt i was
walking with a
partner in fate,

but you ejected
your raw claws.
stretched them into
my wavering throats.

slit me into
parts and portions.
threw my bodies
to fishes in the sea.

beavers are better

i am going
to this world
where they build
and not bomb

i am there
with my mocha
in my hands

legs stretched out
sweet air blowing
off previous dirts

farewell my true
fair weather friends
see no more.

letter to Covid

hey Covid
how are you feeling?

just notice:
i consciously capitalized your name.

i hope
you will get the import of the grammatical illustration.

but wait,
why wield so much power like a lord?

and again,
why seize our o2 with such brazen callousness?

i know
you maybe saying "so what?"

you maybe
saying we deserve what you're serving us right now.

hear this:
you may think you are the Herod of the day

and also
think you are more hard-headed like Pharaoh

but you
forgot how these people went down in ancient history

and your
memory serves you for a limited time period

and that
defines your transient ephemeral nature

let's pray?

let's pray?
and pray you did.

pray when
you ain't
your brother's
keeper.

pray when
you shut
your episcopal
lips

and your
granny, your
mommy, your
kids die

in the
face of
lying lips
and

you pray?

pray, when
your backyard
dries

up from
an inferno
set by
your

accomplice? pray?
is that
all you,
you

whose head
was drenched
with heavenly
oil?
you, you
who put
on holy
robes

like Moses
in the
wilderness? yes,
wilderness

we are
in because
this land
has been
desserted

by blessings
from the
Lord, but
has

been lorded
over by
lawless lords
and faithless
faithfuls

who have
been led
astray by
profligate

promiscuous profane priests
who pray
when

they should
tell, tell

the truth
and

expose evil
but they
pray with
their

double lips
betraying those
they're supposed
to shepherd

pray. pray.
pray you
don't meet
God's wrath.

what do you see?

shrimps and seagulls?
whales and yellow tangs?

coconut octopus and Atlantic bluefin tuna?
cephalopods and crustaceans?

amazona sp. and alopex lagopus?
kaffir or chuckwalla?

meteorites or aurorae?
emptiness or fullness?

the great barrier reef or the pyramids of Giza?
reed flute caves or aso rock?

all I see
is God.

woe!

"tell them."
"tell them what?"
"that they are falling off torrential tangent
and have started singing like bragging Babylonians."
"speaking in scattered un-symmetric speeds that no one understands."
"tell them that they are bouncing like unctuous unsteady rubber balls made of slimy gummy substances that sticks to tainted teeth."
"but, their spirits have left sharpened source and their ears no longer receive signals from gaudy gods."
"they now serve gods so foreign and unfair, gods grounded in deceit and sycophancy, gods gone but left ubiquitous imprints."
"don't doubt, just tell them that I've seen several hands they've been dealing my people."
"tell them to take thousand steps back and at nine hundred and ninety-nine step, they should stop and kneel and weep from their hearts."
"at exactly nine hundred and ninety-nine step, they should stop and not look back but give back all they've stolen from my people."
"all booming blood, all basking brain, all that flows from vein to vein, all and nothing should be left out."
"tell them to do this before glowing rain starts." "for if glorious rain starts, they will be swept away by torrential flood and buried

beneath shallow shame and will be abandoned for violent vultures."

"tell them to do it now, or I will send my fiery fire to incinerate everything in them, including the tiniest in them and anything that will be left of their tattered souls."

"I will, yes I will unscrew their base and dilapidate them like a dynamo to a rocky mountain."

"I will have no mercy for they've been spreading hate on my people and felt untouchable."

"tell them not to remind me of piety pogrom, or the drain pipe white elephant projects, or the ghosting games, or every unconscionable thing they've done under this sun."

"tell them."

as it was in the beginning

to kill another's joy is an illustration of one's insecurity.

to kill one's joy is to incinerate one's inner being.

to kill covetous inner being is to kill both sweetened joy and bubbly being.

blurry countess in the canyon

she was once a psychedelic peeress
catcalls came from inappropriate paramour
her beauty blazed across glazing sea
she was once like a horse in an open country: a horse which never bumbled but throttled through thoroughfares within and between.
her outside curvatures has been derailed by temporary derangement: an eternal transgression that will trail unborn generations and tingle ears that may hear it when history hisses in hovering future.
but, boomerang brought to fore some of her rough edges of yore like water spirit, her pasts bounce back repeatedly in her wrinkled face.
her hair carries convergence of crisis like a billboard blaring in the air, beckoning for forgiveness.

but, now, her righteousness is like a filthy clay, for many diviners have dumped their delusional dreams upon her.

all are Bolingbrook

No matter where; of comfort no man speak:
Let's talk of graves, of worms, and epitaphs;
Make dust our paper and with rainy eyes
Write sorrow on broad bosom of expansive earth,
Let's choose executors and talk of wills:
And yet not so, for what can we bequeath
Save our deposed bodies to grandiose ground?
Our lands, our lives and all are Bolingbroke's,
And nothing can we call our own but death
And that small model of bold barren earth
Which serves as paste and cover to our bones.
For God's sake, let us sit upon gangly ground
And tell sad stories of dire death of kings;
How some have been deposed; some slain in war,
Some haunted by giant ghosts they have deposed;
Some poison'd by their wives: some sleeping kill'd;
All murder'd: for within horrible hollow crown
That rounds many mortal temples of a king
Keeps Death his court and there trounced antic sits,
Scoffing his state and grinning at his pomp,
Allowing him a breath, a little scene,
To monarchize, be fear'd and kill with looks,
Infusing him with self and vain conceit,
As if this flesh which walls about our life,

Were brass impregnable, and humour'd thus
Comes at vast last and with a little pin
Bores through his castle wall, and farewell king!
Cover your heads and mock not flesh and blood
With solemn reverence: throw away respect,
Tradition, form and ceremonious duty,
For you have but mistook me all this while:
I live with bread like you, feel want,
Taste grief, need friends: subjected thus,
How can you say to me, I am a king?

sifter (1)

I've come to loosen
you (the chaff)
from egregious grain. To
spread your bare (naked)
brains on the concrete
floor, and
beat you with a flail. The
nails so pointed and piercing
that it will jerk (throw)
you into atmospheric air and
rake you away
by a strong, strange indecent
nor'easter from
northeast side.

And, you will come
wrecking
into waiting swathers so
ready to make mush of you
like shredders and
clutter paperworks. But
there will be no
augers to move
your drenched (dead) body

in (the room) and
out (cemetery). But
your one (only)
balm is a Man who
stood in gap for you.

sifter (11)

descending down
with indecent
parochial hate
and age-long
wired wrath.
to wreck
the weak,
empty the
open tanks
of the
poor, rain
tears across
forlorn faces
and tear
down their
safety nets.
crumble the
humble, raise
disciples who
will do
more works.
divide the
land, separate
superior from

the less,
let open
floodgates of
untruths into
Christiandom, and
pit one
against the
other to
attain this
mammonic mission.

sifter (iii)

Is so visibly invincible, yet cracks athletic walls
of impregnable pregnancies in broad daylight
with well known assistance but with a stance
that draws up followers to his fold with no
canvassing. He has less tolerance for foreign
bodies who come to add inaudible voices
to an already crowded cult of cultures.
with so much hate, he indecently exposes
what has long been hidden under osmotic
rocky
mountains and buried in unkind monumental avalanche
became available for most to know he is
one of them and speaks like them. He consciously
collude with self-declared incorruptible
judges,
those he knows will easily succumb
to
his openly known deceptions but are
willing
partners in this marriage of the un-comfortables
and uncertainties. Yet, the two dance this
macabre song for a very ineffective derailed
long time and ate from the same plate where
deceit, division, and derision are all served.

i don't know how to ride a bike

"little by little,"
an anonymous writer writes,
"says a thoughtful child."
i will buy punctual patience of an ox
and put it on as my helmet.
i will borrow heels as strong as a super man's
and burrow powdery pedals one step at a time.
i will run as fast as mild molasses
just as if this world will never come to an end.
my neck will be stretched straight as an ostrich, not looking left nor right.
neighbors cheers will fly pass my ears.
honking and thumbs up will not be acknowledged.
just as i wasn't born with a computer but i turned out to be one who unmasks one, i will bring out my big heart and bend my knees one sec per sec.

all these years

our hearts were hot within
peace vacated verandas between
most walked about like shadows,
suffered sorrowful plague of fervent folly
and slept on concretes so low
and drank despicably outlandish dupery
we were in miry clays with feet unestablished,
unable to sing satirical new greatness song because we were wizened
wondrous works of old absquatulated
in debasing words of now
with lips restrained we could not declare derisive new norm deformed
innumerable evils surrounding our surroundings
iniquities numbering more than haggard hairs in our heads over ran our senses
Monday morning mutual confusion ran reckless on funky freeways of awesome airwaves
bed of illness littered around many hallways
whispering like watered whistling pine tree, men sold their balls for a dime
we panted like a deer to wandering water brooks and found no drip to quench our aching taste for all these years.
salty psalm

cast off
put to shame
given us up
scattered us
sold us
next to nothing
a reproach
to our neighbors
all around us,
a derision
a byword
among nerdy nations
shaking of heads
among pious peoples
a dishonor
to this honorable
all these
have come upon
us all
all these years.

as you go into...

may the darkness sweep you
into gnashing eternity
let brisk boiling of your heart rage effusively and drown your
fiendish footsteps
let vociferous vile that came from within your rotten mouth push
you away like a whirlwind
like maniacal muzzle which you triggered, let pricking pellets
pierce through your head and paralyze you
for your wicked heart, you shall be mute with silence and your
sorrow spikes soar.

wounded duck

i see
a duck
a wounded
duck who
shot herself
in her
foot, not
once, not
twice but
multiple times.
i see
a duck
who thinks
she is
a lame
duck, but
not knowing
what waits
for her
in days
and years
to come.
i see
a wounded

duck, who
put pristine
sharp knife
in her
rotund tummy
yet, kept
running red
lights with
so many
breakage behind
her trunk
and millions
cheer and
gear her
up to
the next
red light.
i see
a wounded
duck whose
mouth spread
unspeakable and
unthinkable all
opposed to
her existence,
all pointing
backwards against
her and

ready to
erupt incinerate
extinguish efface
this bad
taste in
the walls
of history.

i see many universe

i see many universe in this one universe
and in this one universe are multiple universes
each speaking in different tongues
each taking directions fitting their footsteps
cracking coiled walls that have kept them in
exhuming age-long sentiments hidden in-between verses of strict holy book
for, if you remember, this tool was employed then
a clever ploy to ownership of what-you-can't-create
but this has been dug way too into weak bones
like an intramuscular intravenous
and allowed to spread so contagiously like a novel virus
yet, heralded by adept followers of chief priests who molds minds to their tastes
thus, dividing kind kingdom even further away from gullible disjointed universes.

in the spirit, the spirit

in the spirit, the spirit
yet cloud of darkness, from Hedes
uncountable demons by Red sea, Sea of Galilee
and imported angels, African angels

under brash belly of our scrotum
lays dark tiny soldier ants
under burst bottom of our tongues
parades poisonous noticeable adders in green grass

voluptuous self-serving serpents
with piously painted parochial voices
yet, tainted in words and deeds
that will stick to and stench their trails.

half staff (1)

i meander through each capitol
near each painted pole of woes
and see pure pains in each of them
mere mirage of onlookers

the teardrops from each passing eye
the heart wreck of each sailing soul
the cleft tightening of each mourning mouth
all tells me plain pain in them

in every heart of every man
in every eyes of every child
in every head of thinking souls
are sighs and sorrows of the nonce

how her headlamps quickly dimmed
darkness ruling on church lamps
with all high hues and all clear cries
all they hear are own voices

yet i meander through their hearts
through the troubled eyes of all
all pieces of torn hearts
and hopeless homes of homelessness.

half staff (2)

let them die
and we flag
the flag at
half for them.
let them be
killed so we
can tell their
own that we
put them in
thoughts and prayers
let their kids
make the bombs
and take them
to the capitol
and we stay
enclosed by the
big walls and
watch their stupidity
play out in
full day nudity
let them expire
so we can
call them heroes
of our time

let them die
for the coin
has flipped and
it is now
their own turn.

to you all

raise the roof
but do not goof
for we have them in the room.

the list of whom
have staked their lives
just for us to have no hives.

tip the drums to scream and say
"heroes you are, and this we say."
we pray you make the history list,

who laid the ground
for this fat hound
who messed up all sowed in the land.

but now is time to sing for joy
we've cried away all tears in the eyes
it's been a year not to replay.

For Dr. Boris, Emeka Orji, you flung the flag of Banner Health.
and Fauci, the wise great one, who turned 80.
and to his wife, the patient dog.

for Sanjay, the suave Gupta, a real surgeon
who's not like those who play it hard
for us all to have herd hearts.

let's rejoice for that is past
and not recoil the dark few years
when everyday was full of f…!

Dr. A, my sweet sister
who wears hats of wife et al
and preach the word for all to hear.

Arlene Ramirez who lost her dad
but still was there to save others
what a year this year has been!

Aida Tekle a full time nurse. all
my classmates at Metro State
who never slept throughout this time.

Kerry Craig Spirals
Elizabeth Gill Okin
Michelle Sprow Countryman

Heather Pine and Steve Costanzo
Steve Gerrio and Adelita Campbell
Amy Piagentini and Chris Orme.

many of you,
all of us,
pioneers we were, pioneers we'll be.

a pensive phase
frenetic frame
the timbrel stung
and screamed a dirge

but blown away by white Christmas
which ushered in a filtered dust
the type which fills an o2 jar
with fresh beginning and no more gasps.
not done yet
we have Pfizer
and another called Moderna
both saviors to modern day.

now, i know mRNA
renewal of my lung and life
or something that I don't know

all I care is no more gasps
and no more gaffes from sycophants
who care so less for you and i
but let's give cheers to caregivers

our lifesavers in modern times.

no amen

and wise world was made flesh
and they submerged in warm wind with whim
and all her glory was lost
as they pursued vainglory and lust

then when...

this is when i
hate this thing-life.
when I see many
moon dropping on my
head and brats circle
around a bald man
who sits on a
wooden rocking chair telling
tales made by him.

this is what I hate:
that we have all
abandoned our yam porridge
and chased after marmalade
made with unfamiliar taste
jammed into our tastebuds
unlike smiling days of
old when we soaked
tubers into spicy red
oil and nodded our
sweating heads in approval.

this is why I hate
all these things-life

for we cannot change
clicking clock hands to
start when we want
and stop when we
are not moving forward
for we have to
move along with thoughtful
tick tock of life
or die when its
batteries have all died.

www.ingramcontent.com/pod-product-compliance
Lightning Source LLC
Chambersburg PA
CBHW031310060426
42444CB00033B/1158